CORPORATE AMERICA

AMAZON

Joy Gregory

LIGHTBOX
openlightbox.com

LIGHTBOX

Go to
www.openlightbox.com
and enter this book's
unique code.

ACCESS CODE

LBU69744

Lightbox is an all-inclusive digital solution for the teaching and learning of curriculum topics in an original, groundbreaking way. Lightbox is based on National Curriculum Standards.

STANDARD FEATURES OF LIGHTBOX

AUDIO High-quality narration using text-to-speech system

ACTIVITIES Printable PDFs that can be emailed and graded

SLIDESHOWS Pictorial overviews of key concepts

VIDEOS Embedded high-definition video clips

WEBLINKS Curated links to external, child-safe resources

TRANSPARENCIES Step-by-step layering of maps, diagrams, charts, and timelines

INTERACTIVE MAPS Interactive maps and aerial satellite imagery

QUIZZES Ten multiple choice questions that are automatically graded and emailed for teacher assessment

KEY WORDS Matching key concepts to their definitions

Contents

Introduction

Amazon.com is the world's largest online **retailer**. Nicknamed the "Everything Store," it is also one of the top 10 largest retailers in the world. Founded and headquartered in Seattle, Washington, the company sells and ships **merchandise** to consumers and businesses across the globe.

Amazon designs and makes many of the products it sells. For other products, it acts as a third-party seller, carrying other companies' goods on the Amazon website. While some of these third parties handle their own shipping, others send their products to Amazon warehouses called fulfillment centers. Amazon has more than 70 fulfillment centers across the United States. The largest is 1.2 million square feet (111,484 square meters) in area. That is about the same size as 28 football fields.

Amazon serves more than
19.5 million
customers every day.

An Amazon warehouse worker can walk more than
10 miles
(16 kilometers)
per day
when picking orders.

Amazon's third-party sellers come from every U.S. state and more than
130 countries.

Amazon lists **369 million**
different products for sale
on its website.

Amazon started as an online bookseller. The company now also operates physical bookstores in key locations across the United States.

amazon

Founding Date	Became Public	Opening Price	Stock Symbol
1994	May 1997	$18.00 USD	Nasdaq: AMZN

Beginnings

Amazon is the brainchild of **entrepreneur** Jeffrey P. Bezos. Born in Albuquerque, New Mexico, on January 12, 1964, Bezos was an imaginative child who grew up building electrical gadgets and machines in his parents' home. When Bezos was a teenager, his family moved to Miami, Florida. While attending high school in Florida, Bezos launched his first business, an educational summer camp for children.

During high school, Bezos developed a strong interest in computers. He graduated from Princeton University in 1986 with a degree in electrical engineering and computer science. Bezos went on to work at several companies in New York City. In 1990, he became the youngest senior vice president at a Wall Street **investment firm**.

Inspired by industry trends that showed the rapid growth of internet use by individuals and companies, Bezos left Wall Street in 1994 and moved to Seattle. It was here that he developed an online bookstore called Amazon.com. Working from his garage, Bezos hired a few employees to help him build the **e-commerce** site. Within 30 days, Amazon had customers in 45 countries. A month later, company sales were at $20,000 a week.

Princeton University was founded in 1746 as the College of New Jersey. Today, it is considered one of the country's top universities.

Amazon.com began trading on the Nasdaq Stock Market in 1997. The following year, the company began to **diversify** its product offerings to include CDs, videos, electronics, clothing, and toys. It also started to develop third-party sales agreements with businesses that wanted to list their products on Amazon's site. Annual sales at Amazon grew from $510,000 in 1995 to almost $136 billion in 2016. By November 2017, Bezos had a personal **net worth** of more than $100 billion, making him one of the richest people in the world.

"We've had three big ideas at Amazon that we've stuck with for 18 years, and they're the reason we're successful: Put the customer first. Invent. And be patient."

– Jeff Bezos,
Amazon Founder

Corporate Timeline

Amazon has come a long way from its modest beginnings as a pioneer in e-commerce. From its beginning as a bookstore, it now sells a multitude of other products, ranging from electronics to clothing. The multibillion-dollar business also includes a fresh food delivery service.

1995

A Website Launches
In its first 30 days of business, Amazon.com sells books to people living in all 50 states.

1997

Going Public
Amazon **stocks** begin trading on the Nasdaq Stock Market. The company is worth $438 million.

1998

E-Sales Expand
The company starts adding new product categories, including music, toys, clothes, and electronics.

2000

The Everything Store
Third-party sales begin, and a new **logo** suggests Amazon is the place to buy everything from A to Z.

2001

Recording a Profit
Amazon records its first quarterly **profit** at the end of the year.

2002

In the Clouds
The company introduces Amazon Web Services (AWS), allowing others to access the technology on which Amazon run its online business.

2007

Gadgets for Sale
Amazon releases its e-reader, Kindle. Four years later, Kindle Fire, a tablet, hits the market.

2007

Amazon Gets Fresh
Amazon opens its first online fresh food delivery service in Seattle.

2012

Robots in Action
Amazon buys a robotics company for $775 million. A year later, the company reveals plans for drone deliveries.

2014

Echo Arrives
Echo, a hands-free device that responds to voice commands, hits the market.

2017

A Tasty Addition
Amazon buys Whole Foods, an upscale grocery chain with more than 460 stores in the United States, Canada, and Great Britain.

Amazon Today

No matter where they are in the world, today's online shoppers are likely to find themselves browsing Amazon's website. Anyone with internet access can use the site to compare prices and customer reviews on a multitude of products. They can then order these items for delivery to their home or office. Approximately 43 percent of all online trade in the United States now goes through Amazon.

By 2017, Amazon's success in attracting buyers in North and South America, Asia, Europe, and Australia pushed its corporate stock to more than $900 a **share**. Amazon continues to look for ways to improve its service to the global marketplace. As part of those efforts, several Amazon websites offer language options. The U.S. site, for example, is available in English and Spanish, the Canadian site has a French option, and the German site is also available in Turkish.

Amazon's high market value reflects its diverse business interests. Amazon's most profitable division, Amazon Web Services (AWS), sells internet-based business services. AWS is a world leader in **cloud computing**. It lets companies access, use, and store data and programs on the internet. With more than 1 million customers, this arm of Amazon generates more than $10 billion in **revenue** annually. Amazon also owns more than 40 **subsidiaries**, including Internet Movie Database (IMDb), an entertainment review site, Shelfari, a book review site, and Audible.com, which sells digital audiobooks. The company also sells its own line of products under its AmazonBasics banner.

People visiting the IMDb database can access information on more than 3.5 million movies, television shows, and other entertainment programs.

"We see our customers as invited guests to a party, and we are the hosts. It's our job every day to make every important aspect of the customer experience a little bit better."

– Jeff Bezos,
Amazon **Chief Executive Officer (CEO)**

A World of Amazon

Amazon is a global business, with operations all around the world. While much of its focus remains in the United States, the company has **software** development centers, customer service centers, and fulfillment centers on almost every continent.

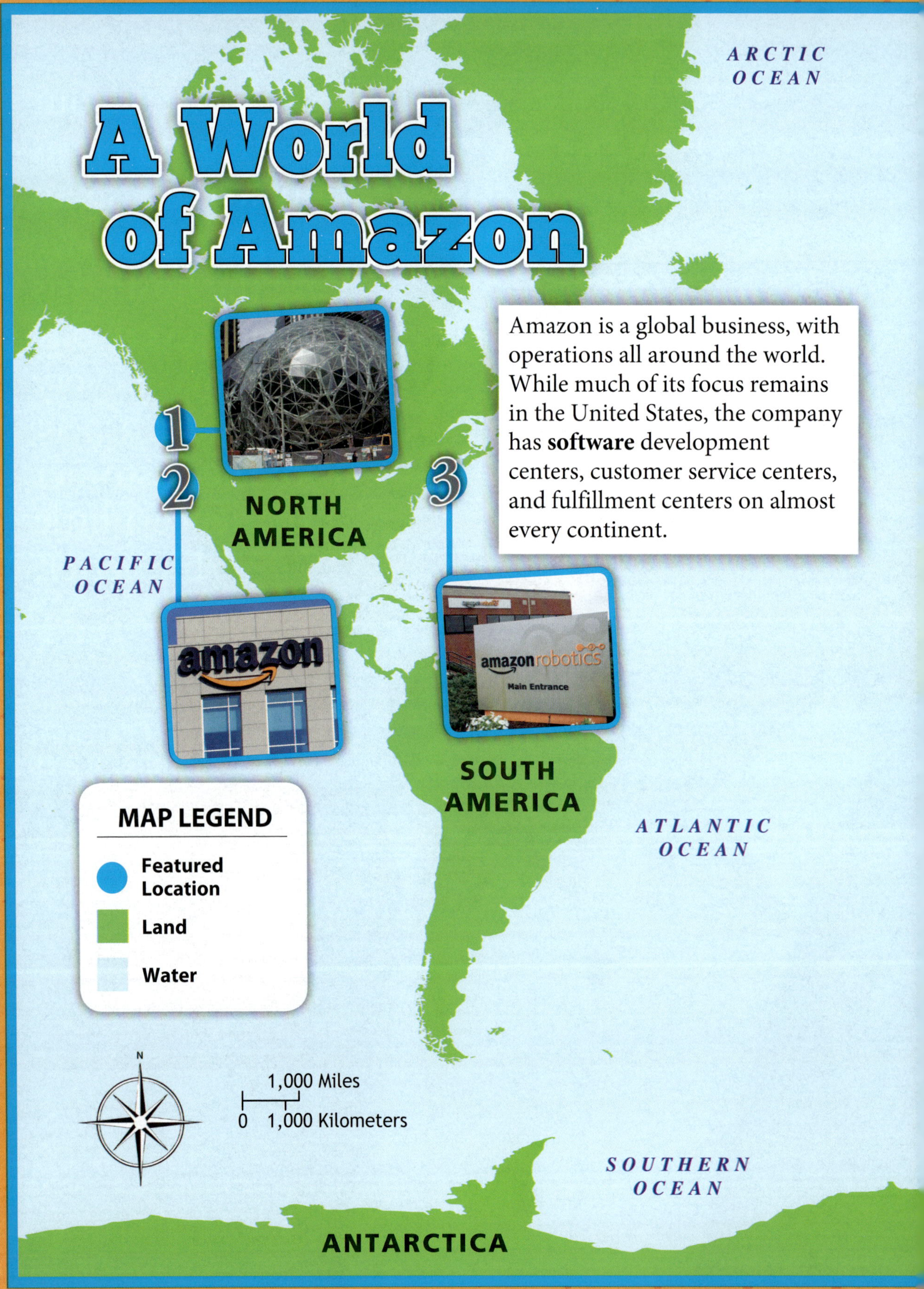

1 **Corporate Headquarters** Amazon's corporate headquarters is located in Seattle, Washington. Currently under construction, it will be a three-tower complex when completed in 2019.

2 **Lab126** Amazon's research and development company is located in California's San Francisco Bay Area. Lab126 engineers Amazon devices, including Fire tablets, Kindle e-readers, and Amazon Echo.

3 **Amazon Robotics** This Amazon subsidiary is headquartered near Boston, Massachusetts. It develops the technology used to store and then locate and move products for shipping inside Amazon fulfillment centers.

4 **European Headquarters** Amazon's European operations are based in Luxembourg. Located in Luxembourg City, the office employs more than 1,000 people.

5 **Kanagawa Fulfillment Center** Japan's Kanagawa prefecture is home to the country's largest Amazon fulfillment center. The five-story building covers more than 2.1 million square feet (195,100 sq. m).

Branding Amazon

To be successful, Amazon needed a **brand** that would attract buyers who were used to shopping in physical stores. That brand had to give consumers a reason to try online shopping. More importantly, it had to turn first-time e-commerce shoppers into repeat customers. Amazon did that with a branding strategy that highlights price, selection, and convenience.

Price Low prices are key to the Amazon brand. From the beginning, the company purposefully developed a reputation for selling products at low prices. The company ensures customers understand the deals it is offering them by including side-by-side price comparisons on the Amazon website. Amazon's third-party sellers are also keen on selling their goods at lower prices than those found in retail stores. This drives even more people to the Amazon website.

Selection Product choice is another way Amazon distinguishes itself in the consumer market. Amazon sells a larger variety of products and brand names than traditional retailers or other online stores. It also adds thousands of new products to its **inventory** every day. With dozens of departments to choose from, consumers can shop Amazon for items ranging from fine art to groceries to sports equipment. Within many of its departments, Amazon lists more than 10 million products.

Convenience Convenience is one of the main reasons online buyers keep returning to Amazon.com. Instead of making consumers search for items by brand name, Amazon groups merchandise into categories. Shoppers simply go to the category and find the specific product page for the item they want to buy. Product pages are designed to make it easy for shoppers to compare prices and product reviews. Each product page also provides shipping options. This focus on convenience also extends to product returns. Aware that online shoppers may be nervous about buying a product they have not seen, Amazon makes it easy for buyers to return products. Some returns even qualify for free shipping. Amazon also tracks customer complaints and uses this information to improve its services.

amazon

Company Name

Amazon.com is named after the Amazon River, one of the longest rivers in the world. The name was chosen to reflect the company's size and reach. When Amazon.com launched, internet search results were presented alphabetically. That also made Amazon a good choice.

Company Logo

The company logo features an arrow that points from "A" to "Z." It promotes the idea that Amazon sells everything. The arrow is also designed to look like the smile of a happy customer.

Company Slogan

Amazon aims to be "Earth's most customer-centric company." The **slogan** reinforces Amazon's commitment to pleasing its customers.

The Art of Selling

Amazon has always been at the forefront of the industry when it comes to innovation. Its early entry into e-commerce is proof of the company's innovative spirit. As a forward-thinking company, Amazon continues to develop programs and concepts that will meet its customers' needs and encourage both continuing and new business.

Amazon Prime Launched in 2005, Amazon Prime is a membership-based **loyalty program** that encourages customers to buy more products from Amazon.com. In return for paying a monthly or annual fee, Prime members get free and faster shipping, and access to special services and deals. The details of Amazon Prime differ from country to country. In the United States, more than 80 million people subscribe to Prime. For a flat fee, Prime Pantry customers in the contiguous states can even have grocery, household, and pet care items delivered to their homes.

Amazon Stores Amazon opened its first physical stores in 2014. Amazon Pop-Up is a kiosk-type store located in the aisles of traditional retail malls across the United States. These stores give the company an opportunity to sell its electronic devices, including Kindle, Echo, and Fire tablets, in a more traditional retail setting. By 2017, Amazon had 29 Pop-Up stores in 15 states. The first physical Amazon bookstore, Amazon Books, opened in 2015. Within two years, 10 U.S. cities were home to the stores, with plans to open even more in the next few years. Amazon Books sells books that get four or more stars from readers on Amazon.com. The stores also sell Amazon devices.

The first Kindle e-reader hit the market in *2007*. **Priced at $399 USD**, it sold out **within 6 hours**.

The U.S. site for Amazon.com lists **45 categories of goods**.

On its **busiest day in 2016**, Amazon.com sold **636 items per second**.

Competitors

Amazon conducts its business in a highly competitive global marketplace. On the retail front, some of Amazon's biggest competitors are traditional department stores. Other retailers compete with Amazon solely in the world of e-commerce. In cloud computing, Amazon competes against the giants of the tech industry.

Walmart

STOCK SYMBOL nyse: WMT

Walmart generates more revenue per year than any other company in the United States. Established in 1962 by Samuel Moore Walton, Walmart is based in Bentonville, Arkansas. Worldwide, Walmart has more than 11,600 stores. Online and in stores, Walmart's products range from electronics to groceries to clothing. Stores also feature photography, pharmacy, optical, and automobile services.

Alibaba.com

STOCK SYMBOL nyse: BABA

Based in Hangzhou, China, Alibaba Group was founded in 1999 by a group of 18 businessmen. The company runs Taobao Marketplace, an online shopping website. It has ownership in the social media sites Youku Tudou and Weibo as well. Alibaba also operates Tmall.com, a global online website for vendors selling into the Chinese marketplace.

Microsoft

STOCK SYMBOL nasdaq: MSFT

Located in Redmond, Washington, Microsoft was founded by Bill Gates and Paul Allen in 1975. The company develops software and **hardware** for computers and smart devices, such as tablets and phones. Microsoft operates in three key areas. These are personal computing, business processes and productivity, and cloud computing.

Comparison Chart

Businesses keep records to track their **assets**, **liabilities**, profits, and losses. Companies use this data to guide expansion and cost-cutting decisions. Investors use the information to help them decide where to invest their money. They will also refer to a company's **market capitalization** to gauge public confidence in the business.

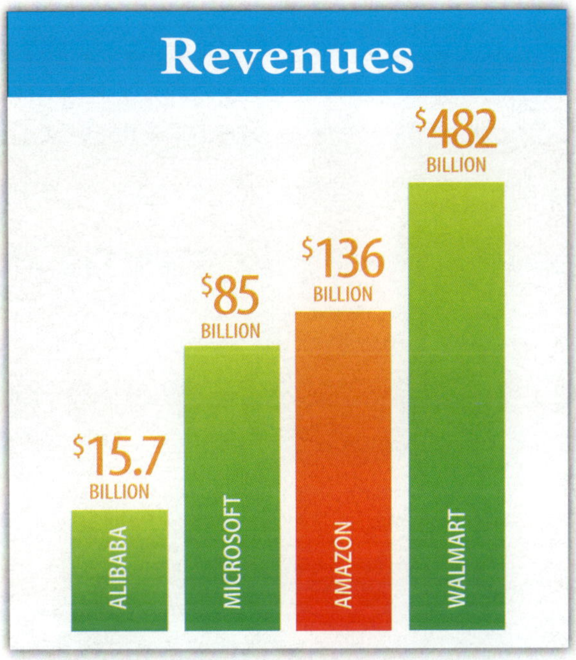

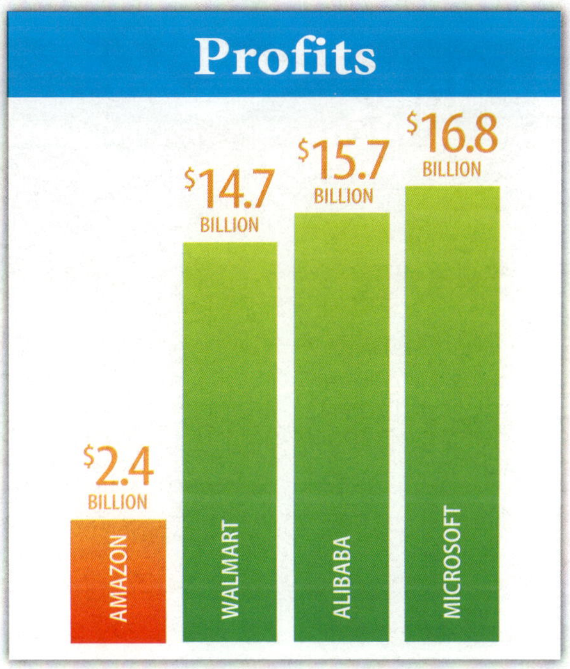

2016 Figures

Innovation and Technology

Amazon Echo

Released in 2014, Amazon Echo has changed how people receive and use information in their homes. The hands-free device connects to the Alexa Voice Service. When users want something done, they issue the command through Alexa. The service allows them to play music, send and receive messages, make phone calls, and get information about news, sports scores, and the weather. It can also operate home devices such as garage doors, lights, and thermostats.

The Smart Store

Amazon opened its first Amazon Go store in 2016. A cashless convenience-style store for Amazon employees in Seattle, Amazon Go lets shoppers pay for their purchases using an **app**. The stores make use of Amazon's cloud computing, machine learning, voice control, and logistics expertise. In the future, Amazon Go stores will be open to the public. The technology used to operate Amazon Go may eventually be sold to other companies.

Robotic Workflow

Amazon's website makes it easy for consumers to place orders. Once those orders arrive at a fulfillment center, much of the work, and almost all of the lifting, is handled by robots. Engineered by employees in Amazon's robotics division, these robots help locate and then move items from warehouse shelves to staff, who double-check that the picked items match the customer's order. Other robots help workers send products for labeling and shipping.

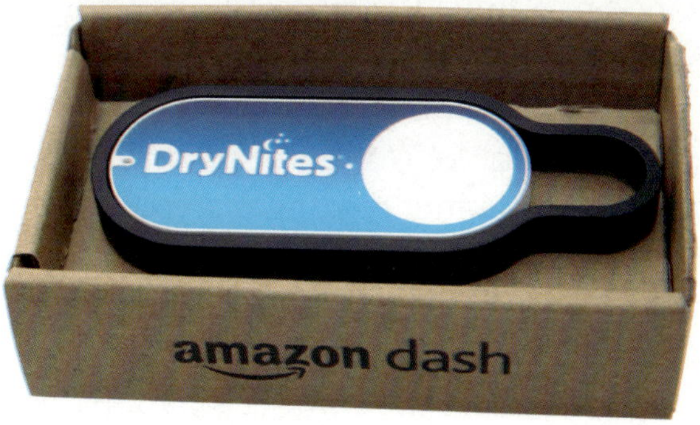

Dash Buttons

Amazon has provided its Prime customers with a shortcut for reordering favorite items. Dash Buttons can be set up on a customer's computer or mobile device. Each button links to a specific Amazon product. With a simple tap on a button or click of a computer mouse, the order is sent to a fulfillment center for processing. Dash Button users also have the option of buying a small wifi-enabled electronic device from Amazon that is solely for sending Dash orders.

Giving Back

Corporate **philanthropy** programs link companies to certain causes or charities. Amazon's corporate giving targets the communities where its consumers and employees live. Projects supported by Amazon range from poverty reduction to programs that increase literacy. Amazon customers can also make a difference through the company's AmazonSmile program. It allows them to donate a portion of their purchase price to charity.

Mary's Place In 2016, Amazon gave a homeless shelter permission to move into a building owned by the company in downtown Seattle. The following year, the company announced that the shelter would move into six stories of a new office tower Amazon is building. When it opens in 2020, Mary's Place will house about 65 families. The shelter will have a separate entrance and elevator, and shelter residents will be allowed to bring their pets.

Kindle Reading Fund Amazon developed its Kindle Reading Fund to help improve children's literacy. The goal of the fund is to make reading materials accessible to people all over the world. Amazon's focus has been on providing reading materials in a digital format. To accomplish this, the company has donated thousands of Kindle e-readers and Fire tablets to schools, libraries, and hospitals across the globe. The company also works with organizations that share its goals. These include Worldreader, which promotes literacy in developing countries, and the U.S National Parent Teacher Association.

FareStart In 2017, Amazon announced that it was donating more than 25,000 square feet (2,300 sq. m) of space in its Seattle office to FareStart. This charity provides job training in food services to people from disadvantaged backgrounds. The goal is to help them gain the skills needed to enter the job market. FareStart plans to use the space Amazon donated to open a full-service restaurant, three cafés, a coffee shop, a catering space, and training classrooms.

In 2015, **Amazon** gave more than **500** **U.S. military children** gifts from their holiday wish lists.

More than **100,000 charities** have received money from **AmazonSmile**.

Mary's Place will provide homes for more than **200 homeless people**.

Into the Future

Now a dominant e-commerce player across most online retail categories, Amazon shows no signs of slowing down. Amazon's corporate share price more than doubled between 2015 and 2017, and first quarter sales for 2017 hit a record $35.7 billion. Industry insiders predict Amazon could be the first **public company** to be worth $1 trillion.

Amazon's biggest challenge for the future is to stay ahead of its rivals. One of the main threats to Amazon's growth comes from competition in the cloud computing industry. Amazon Web Services (AWS) currently has 34 percent of the cloud computing market, but Microsoft, Google, and IBM are building market share. AWS generates about 10 percent of the money Amazon makes. Amazon's focus on selling what customers want to buy is expected to fuel continued growth. By early 2017, the company had 300 million user accounts around the world.

The company is taking steps to show customers that Amazon is community-minded. It is increasing its philanthropic work and its investment in projects that help the company be more environmentally sustainable. While Amazon's corporate giving programs are especially robust in Seattle, the company is gradually extending its reach globally. It also continues to conduct research into ways of reducing the company's environmental footprint. Much of this research is focused on developing sustainable technologies and improving packaging to produce less waste.

In 2017, Amazon opened its largest Indian fulfillment center in Hyderabad. The center spans 400,000 square feet (37,161 sq. m).

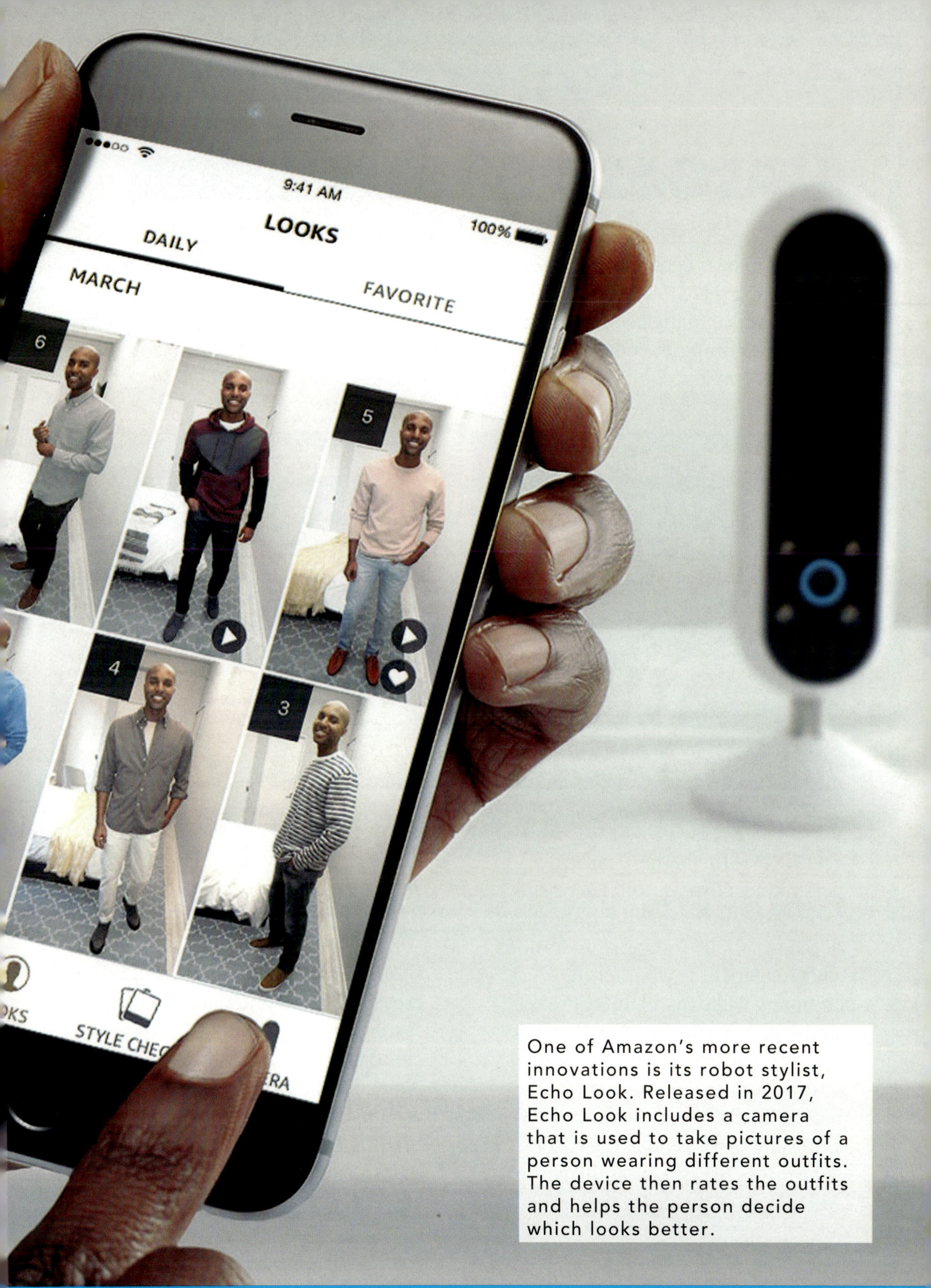

One of Amazon's more recent innovations is its robot stylist, Echo Look. Released in 2017, Echo Look includes a camera that is used to take pictures of a person wearing different outfits. The device then rates the outfits and helps the person decide which looks better.

Careers at Amazon

Amazon depends on thousands of employees to make its business work. Careers at Amazon range from the executives who work in the U.S. head office to the people who update Amazon websites, pack items for shipping, and write computer code for Amazon's cloud computing business. Amazon likes to say its employees all work towards a single goal—customer satisfaction.

Chief Executive Officer

$1.7 million per year

The CEO is the highest-ranked person in a corporation. He or she is responsible for making important decisions about company operations. This may include whether the company will expand, merge, or sell some of its assets. The CEO usually consults with the company's **board of directors** and management team before finalizing any action. Working alongside these people, the CEO determines the direction the company will take over the next few years.

Computer Engineer

$65,000–$147,000 per year

Amazon employs computer engineers with a variety of specialties. Some design, build, and maintain the computer systems that run online shopping at Amazon.com. Others create, operate, and update the systems used to run the company's cloud computing business. Amazon fulfillment centers also employ computer engineers to maintain the robotics equipment that makes fulfillment centers safe and efficient.

Warehouse Associate

$28,000 per year

Amazon fulfillment centers rely on their warehouse associates to handle incoming and outgoing merchandise. Some associates unload shipments from trucks. Others put merchandise onto warehouse shelves. Aided by robotic technology, Amazon "pickers" locate ordered items on the shelves and send them to "packers." Packers prepare the items for shipping.

Safety Specialist

$57,000–$71,000 per year

Amazon's safety specialists ensure that the work environment is safe for all employees. These workers oversee regular checks of equipment and working conditions. They also help workers comply with the company's safety programs and with all federal and state laws. When new equipment is bought, safety specialists make sure employees receive proper training.

Activity

Amazon adds new products to its website every day. Many of these products come from third-party sellers. Third-party sellers must submit specific information about their product to Amazon. Amazon then uses that information to design a product detail page. That page includes the product name, a picture and description of the product, and the product price.

Imagine that you are a third-party seller and have a product that you think Amazon's customers would like to purchase. Use the questions below to help you develop a product detail page for your product.

1. What is the name of your product?
2. Write a description of your product. What does your product do? How will it help people? What are its main features?
3. What does your product look like? Draw a picture of it to include on your page.
4. How much does your product cost?
5. How quickly can a customer have the product delivered?

Quiz

1 Where is Amazon's corporate headquarters?

2 Who founded Amazon?

3 When Amazon first opened for business, what did it sell?

4 Where are Amazon stocks traded?

5 What is the name of Amazon's e-reader?

6 What is Amazon's nickname?

7 How many subsidiaries does Amazon own?

8 What is Amazon Prime?

9 What kind of product is Echo?

10 Which Amazon program allows its customers to donate part of their purchase price to charity?

Answers

1. Seattle, Washington **2.** Jeff Bezos **3.** Books **4.** Nasdaq Stock Market **5.** Kindle **6.** Everything Store **7.** More than 40 **8.** A membership-based loyalty program **9.** Hands-free device **10.** AmazonSmile

Key Words

app: short for application, a software program used on desktop computers and mobile devices

assets: valuable properties owned by a company or person

board of directors: a group of people who oversee the direction a company is taking

brand: characteristics that serve to identify a particular company

chief executive officer (CEO): the highest-ranking person in a company

cloud computing: storing and accessing data over the internet

diversify: to enlarge or vary a company's range of products

e-commerce: the buying and selling of goods in online markets

entrepreneur: a person who organizes and operates a business

hardware: the physical parts of a computer or electronic device

inventory: a complete list of merchandise on hand

investment firm: a company that invests other people's money to make a profit

liabilities: a company's debts and business costs

logo: a symbol or design used to identify a specific company

loyalty program: a rewards system offered by a company to customers who make frequent purchases

market capitalization: the market value of a company's outstanding shares

merchandise: products to sell

net worth: the amount by which assets exceed liabilities

philanthropy: making life better for other people

profit: money left over after expenses have been met

public company: a company that issues shares traded on at least one stock exchange

retailer: seller of goods

revenue: the amount of money a company receives for goods or services sold over a particular amount of time

share: a unit of ownership in a company

slogan: a distinctive phrase used to identify a specific company or product

software: the programs and other operating information used by a computer

stocks: shares of a company held by a group or individual

subsidiaries: divisions of a larger company

Index

LIGHTBOX

SUPPLEMENTARY RESOURCES

Click on the plus icon found in the bottom left corner of each spread to open additional teacher resources.

- Download and print the book's quizzes and activities
- Access curriculum correlations
- Explore additional web applications that enhance the Lightbox experience

LIGHTBOX DIGITAL TITLES
Packed full of integrated media

VIDEOS

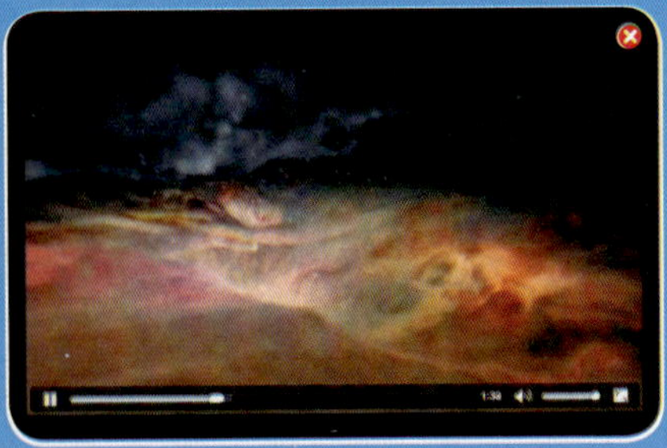

INTERACTIVE MAPS

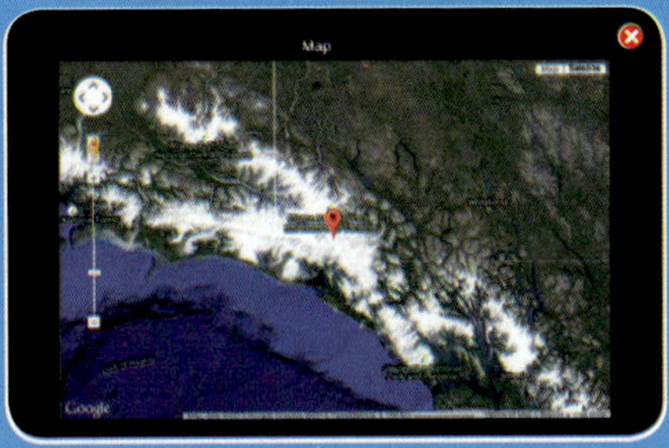

WEBLINKS

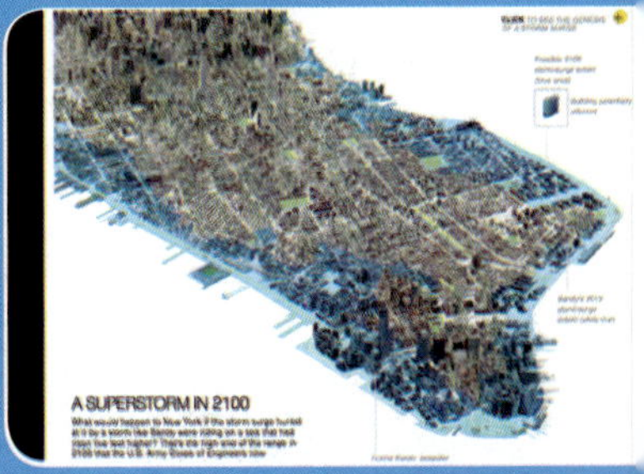

SLIDESHOWS

QUIZZES

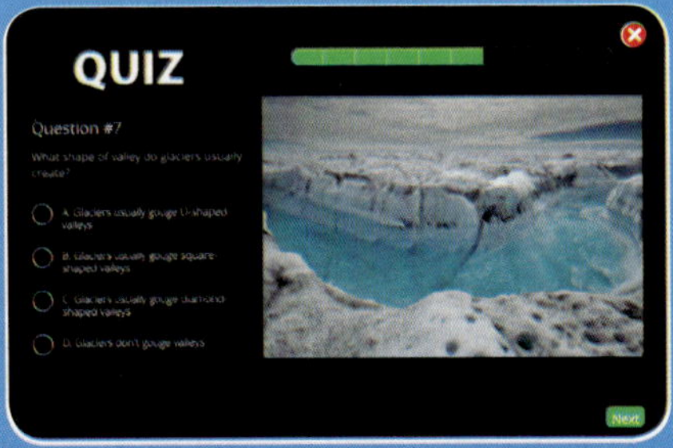

OPTIMIZED FOR
- ✓ TABLETS
- ✓ WHITEBOARDS
- ✓ COMPUTERS
- ✓ AND MUCH MORE!

Published by Smartbook Media Inc.
350 5th Avenue, 59th Floor New York, NY 10118
Website: www.openlightbox.com

Editor: Heather Kissock
Designer: Nick Newton

Library of Congress Cataloging-in-Publication Data
Names: Gregory, Joy, author.
Title: Amazon / Joy Gregory.
Description: New York, NY : Smartbook Media Inc., [2019] | Series: Corporate America | Includes index.
Identifiers: LCCN 2017048291 | ISBN 9781510534933 (Multi-User Ebook) | ISBN 9781510534926 (hard cover : alk. paper)
Subjects: LCSH: Amazon.com (Firm)--Juvenile literature. | Internet bookstores--Juvenile literature. | Electronic commerce--Juvenile literature.
Classification: LCC Z473.A485 G745 2019 | DDC 381/.142065--dc23
LC record available at https://lccn.loc.gov/2017048291

Printed in Brainerd, Minnesota, United States
1 2 3 4 5 6 7 8 9 0 21 20 19 18 17

122017
151217

Photo Credits
Every reasonable effort has been made to trace ownership and to obtain permission to reprint copyright material. The publisher would be pleased to have any errors or omissions brought to its attention so that they may be corrected in subsequent printings. The publisher acknowledges Alamy, Getty Images, iStock, Shutterstock, and Newscom as its primary image suppliers for this title.